Jonathan Reeve Price

Viewing Hokusai
Viewing Mount Fuji

Copyright 2020 by Jonathan Reeve Price

Publisher: The Communication Circle
4704 Mi Cordelia Drive, NW
Albuquerque, NM 87120
www.museumzero.art

Published in the United States of America.
First Publication: 2020
ISBN-10: 0-9719954-7-8
ISBN-13: 978-0-9719954-7-5

Contents ...

Look at that flower with its petals blown back by the wind. Is that not truth itself?

And here, near this woman by Hokusai, look at this bathing scene! Look at these bodies. Can you feel their firmness?

They are made of flesh, but they are described only by their outline. The bold way he defines his subject! Those people taught us how to compose differently.

—Claude Monet

A Note on Method

Metaphor arises when fields collide.
One point pings in several planes at once—
A dust mite from one angle, from another, life.
This painting sits where the Buddhist path
Crosses the floating world, this beautiful illusion.
Uki is floating, yo's the world, and this print, e,
One of the first consumer graphics, paid for
By merchants rising, daimyo's switching
From castle to inn or factory, and rich peasants.
Ukiyo-e!
In Hokusai, Chinese mists blot out
Landscapes so detailed and almost real
That tourists have looked for the spots he sat,
Just to compare the picture to the present.
Loyal and proud, he painted the national icon
In perspective borrowed from the Dutch. Trade
Opened his eyes, and earned his rice. Popular,
he fitted humans into a large, wet land—
Dots in the distance, each distinct.
Flat, but deep, his art quotes
Other art, but looks convincingly strange,
Like a photograph: then, as we examine
A tower, or tree, we see the real dissolve.

View through Waves off the Coast of Kanagawa

Old man rowing,
Crazy for painting,
Name changer,
Shape shifter,
Icon maker,
Worshipping a volcano.

Like a wave
I zoom in, and withdraw,
Like an eye,
I pixelate,
I blur my borders,
And grow perspective.
As poet, though,
I make
Text strings in
Wave lengths,
Catastrophe frozen,
Fractal with foam,
Fear and pity held
Tight as the first cut in
The uncarved block.

View through Waves off the Coast of Kanagawa

Such an islander, he thinks like a fish—
He's swum under these breakers, out
Where you can't touch bottom, to push
Back up. Bang, the wave comes down,
In real seas. But here the death blow
Is suspended—studied—carved in wood.

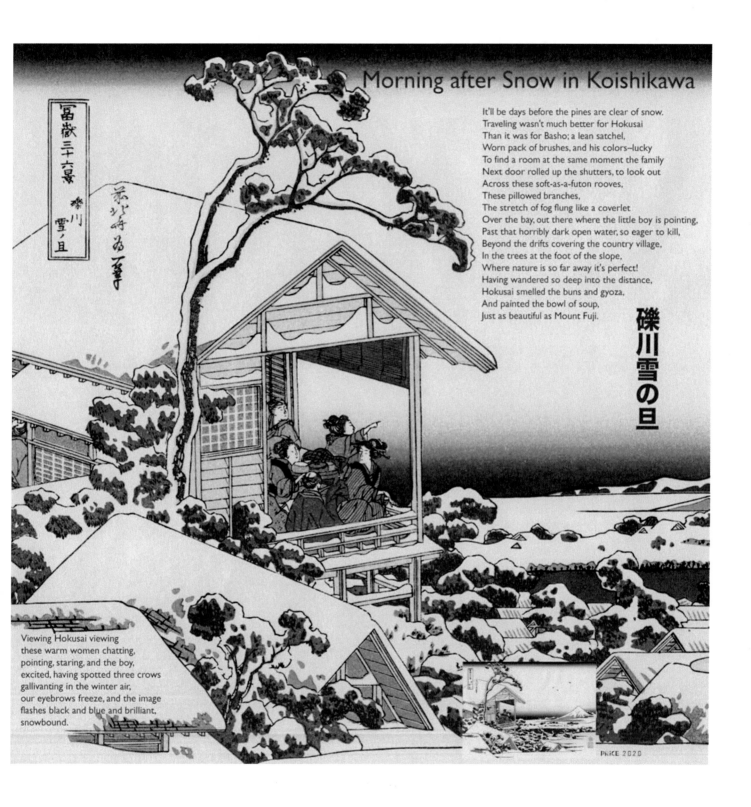

Morning after Snow in Koishikawa

It'll be days before the pines are clear of snow.
Traveling wasn't much better for Hokusai
Than it was for Basho; a lean satchel,
Worn pack of brushes, and his colors–lucky
To find a room at the same moment the family
Next door rolled up the shutters, to look out
Across these soft-as-a-futon rooves,
These pillowed branches,
The stretch of fog flung like a coverlet
Over the bay, out there where the little boy is pointing,
Past that horribly dark open water, so eager to kill,
Beyond the drifts covering the country village,
In the trees at the foot of the slope,
Where nature is so far away it's perfect!
Having wandered so deep into the distance,
Hokusai smelled the buns and gyoza,
And painted the bowl of soup,
Just as beautiful as Mount Fuji.

Viewing Hokusai viewing
these warm women chatting,
pointing, staring, and the boy,
excited, having spotted three crows
gallivanting in the winter air,
our eyebrows freeze, and the image
flashes black and blue and brilliant,
snowbound.

PRICE 2020

Ejiri in Suruga

The trees reach up so high they break the frame,
Convincing us that the mountain still lies behind,
Two slopes, and a crater, all sketched in one line,
A suggestion of a form, a ghost.

Unpainted
Bright water slices into the marsh,
Separating us from
Some far shore, and
Beyond that, an equally
Imaginary shape, a white blank.

Text adds nothing to art, but
this great wind
explodes the message,
blasting pages into the air,
tossing one man's bamboo hat
like an idea lost in passion,
a definition so precise that it destroys
what we intuit, blown away by this
shape-figure, and this uncertain ground.

But this woman's lost her vision,
Hair thrashing, hat gone, her pile
Of papers rippling off, rat-a-tat,
Before she could clap a hand on top,
Gone, the love letters from the samurai,
Lost, the bills and accounts, streaked and
Ruined, the print of the kabuki.
The brushstrokes blur in mid air,
Rain rushing down, pummeling paper
Into the long grass, each blade
Whipping like a furious pen.

PRICE 2020

These folks up front, tangled and twisted,
Bent double against the roar, blown
Nearly off the trail, grab hat and cloth,
Haul in their bags, and stagger on.

Slash, slash, slash,
The zigzagging pathway
Cuts back and forth,
The blankness itself
Leading us, East or West,
by Hokusai's suggestion, Hiroshige.

Like bicycle messengers in New York, these samurai
Gouge flanks, lift up off their horses, jockeying
Through this curve as they leave town, crossing rice paddies,
Toward what? Intense mutterings, perhaps, conspiracies,
Exploding revolt? So quickly forgotten, that reason
They rushed past Sekiya, down to the Sumida.

These marks make rice.
Controlled by delicate outlines,
the pure colors form
horse and rock and tree.
But whiteness makes the indistinct mist
and its source, the road,
lead us back, layer by layer, to
the unnaturally immense Mount Fuji,
impossibly red.

It's too early in the morning
For mist to clear.
And water looks as white as
the moist cold air
Slicing across the scene,
Conveniently providing impenetrable depth,
Like that oddly placed tree, reaching to heaven,
raggedly bent, wiggling like the road.

Sekiya Village on the Sumida River

They ignore this inn sign inviting them to pause.
Take off their bamboo hats, round as wheels.
Uncinch and take some nice rice and hot tea.

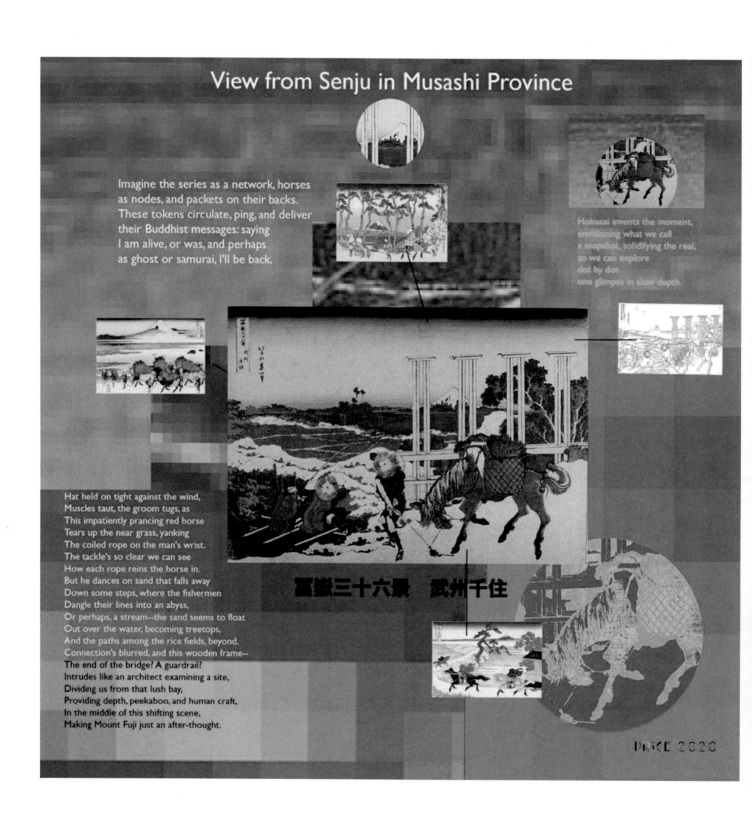

View from Senju in Musashi Province

Imagine the series as a network, horses
as nodes, and packets on their backs.
These tokens circulate, ping, and deliver
their Buddhist messages: saying
I am alive, or was, and perhaps
as ghost or samurai, I'll be back.

Hokusai invents the moment,
envisioning what we call
a snapshot, solidifying the real,
so we can explore
dot by dot
one glimpse in slow depth.

Hat held on tight against the wind,
Muscles taut, the groom tugs, as
This impatiently prancing red horse
Tears up the near grass, yanking
The coiled rope on the man's wrist.
The tackle's so clear we can see
How each rope reins the horse in.
But he dances on sand that falls away
Down some steps, where the fishermen
Dangle their lines into an abyss,
Or perhaps, a stream--the sand seems to float
Out over the water, becoming treetops,
And the paths among the rice fields, beyond.
Connection's blurred, and this wooden frame--
The end of the bridge? A guardrail?
Intrudes like an architect examining a site,
Dividing us from that lush bay,
Providing depth, peekaboo, and human craft,
In the middle of this shifting scene,
Making Mount Fuji just an after-thought.

冨嶽三十六景　武州千住

PRICE 2020

Hodogaya on the Tōkaidō

Painting sky in three broad bands—
These restraining walls separate and emphasize,
Making multiple stage sets, and yet,
By stretching from east to west,
These lines form the staff, the trees
The baseline, and these quivering pedestrians
Raise the raw melody.

Like a decorated curtain, the trees
Arise between us and the smutzig lake,
Isolating the performers here in front of us,
Each trunk a module in the rhythm
Of the open road to the far north.

How personal each traveler is, uniquely
Bending to look in his or her own way:
Introspective, worshipful, itchy, awed, or
Indifferent. Even the horse has his own idea.

Absorbing silence, the far hills
Sit greenly dreaming
Of being a butterfly, no, a hawk,
Anything that can flutter up to become,
In that clean cold air, the crescendo,
A sharp grace note.

Lake Suwa in Shinano

And right there Hokusai grows two trees
Splitting the scene in half, tearing
The sky with wretched twisted trunks,
And branches blasted by updrafts.

How sharp the point, the white
triangle, the tiny hut,
Mount Fuji, a far-off sail.

Both sides of the lake exist
In night blue, not yet awake.

How contemplative this shack on a crag,
So far above the lake we see the ship as a toy.

Hokusai explodes the near,
Stills the far,
And omits the in-between.

We fall from this rock
Hundreds of feet, past
Cliffs we can't see, into
Sheer water—there's
Not even a beach.

Cushion Pine at Aoyama

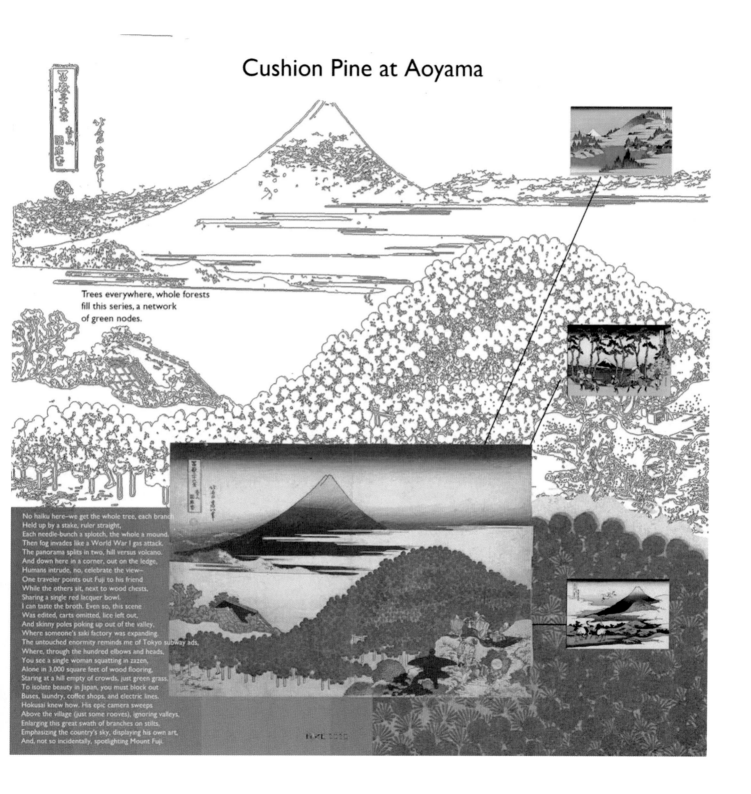

Trees everywhere, whole forests
fill this series, a network
of green nodes.

No haiku here—we get the whole tree, each branch
Held up by a stake, ruler straight,
Each needle-bunch a splotch, the whole a mound.
Then fog invades like a World War I gas attack.
The panorama splits in two, hill versus volcano.
And down here in a corner, out on the ledge,
Humans intrude, no, celebrate the view—
One traveler points out Fuji to his friend
While the others sit, next to wood chests,
Sharing a single red lacquer bowl.
I can taste the broth. Even so, this scene
Was edited, carts omitted, lice left out,
And skinny poles poking up out of the valley,
Where someone's saki factory was expanding.
The untouched enormity reminds me of Tokyo subway ads,
Where, through the hundred elbows and heads,
You see a single woman squatting in zazen,
Alone in 3,000 square feet of wood flooring,
Staring at a hill empty of crowds, just green grass.
To isolate beauty in Japan, you must block out
Buses, laundry, coffee shops, and electric lines.
Hokusai knew how. His epic camera sweeps
Above the village (just some rooves), ignoring valleys,
Enlarging this great swath of branches on stilts,
Emphasizing the country's sky, displaying his own art,
And, not so incidentally, spotlighting Mount Fuji.

At Mishima Pass

Down one slope, and up the next, the goddess runs.
Puffing steam, smoke, and lava tears, as
Thin threads of glass land around
Her dark top–she forms one cloud.
And bounces the others off, the drifters,
Stuck together and bunched like sushi rice.
Quiet as a geisha waiting for the lute,
Half undressed, her nipple hardening,
She puts her moist attention on this tree.

This big hairy phallus erupts from the frame,
High on the ridge, where the travelers rest,
Sip soup, and laugh, trying to ring its trunk.
How active that member, surging
Up without a branch until it hits blue sky.
The rectangle cannot contain it,
Nor this steady cool breeze,
Nor the wind-bleached ground.

Fleas, these peasants scratch around the cypress,
Contemplating the path itself, the bark,
The rocks that resemble thatch–
Not one looking out past the brush,
They miss the emerging sharp breast,
The discretely aroused Mount Fuji.

PRICE 2020

Ushibori in Hitachi

常州牛掘

Cranes, startled, lift up from the marsh.
Without urgency,
More out of habit than fear.
The bay is calm, the snow frozen
On the peak that he never climbed.
He preferred surrounding
Not taking, contemplating without
Itchy fingers. In one stroke
He shows a ghost, like the Ainu tribesmen
Who named it, so absent they are white,
A big blank like that of the bay,
An extinguished Mount Fuji.

No haste here, nothing's broken,
So time
Opens up for chores—
Stacking tatami,
Drying rushes,
Washing the stones for ballast.
The aft deck's been swabbed,
The lacquerware is stowed,
and the crew can snooze.

From the beached boat, the sound
Of a bucket scraping the gunnels, collecting
Bilge, then pouring it over the side.
Still more ripples come in on the port beam,
Never lifting the keel free, but rolling
The reeds, and slipping through the uncaulked gap
In the planks. Listen to the steady sound of water—
Like the raked stones of Ryoanji, and the moss,
Like the spatter of raindrops in the bamboo
Uphill from the Silver Pavilion.
We hear nothing loudly but expect the tide,
Like the big bell outside the temple,
Silent now, but enormous in expectation
With the log up on ropes, ready to be swung,
Gong, into its immense gray cone.

PRICE 2020

17

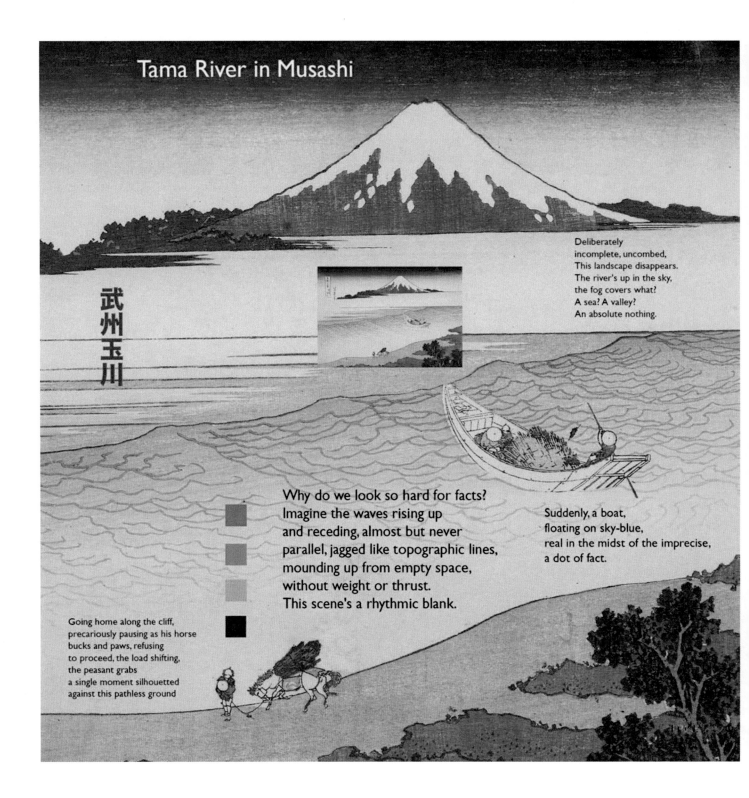

Tama River in Musashi

武州玉川

Deliberately
incomplete, uncombed,
This landscape disappears.
The river's up in the sky,
the fog covers what?
A sea? A valley?
An absolute nothing.

Why do we look so hard for facts?
Imagine the waves rising up
and receding, almost but never
parallel, jagged like topographic lines,
mounding up from empty space,
without weight or thrust.
This scene's a rhythmic blank.

Suddenly, a boat,
floating on sky-blue,
real in the midst of the imprecise,
a dot of fact.

Going home along the cliff,
precariously pausing as his horse
bucks and paws, refusing
to proceed, the load shifting,
the peasant grabs
a single moment silhouetted
against this pathless ground

Sunset across the Ryōgoku Bridge
over the Sumida River at Onmayagashi

Oh my gosh, the Sumida River's as big
As Tokyo Bay—and heavy. The small boats strain
Anchor chains against the current ...
And this enormous bridge, too, all wood
And sweat, arching over the deep waters,
An industrial triumph, a carpenter's high tech,
Advertising nationhood.

Hokusai's so delicate with horizons,
The uneven surfaces indicate house, tree,
Ridge, and hubbub, without disrupting
The line of shore stuff, the far side,
This intriguing other, just out of reach.

Not so magnificent for these passengers,
Tossed up and down near shore, rough stiff waves
Knocking boat and baggage back and forth,
As the oarsman just gets free of the dock.
How many of their great grandchildren
Are stuck in Tokyo traffic today,
Or studiously sleeping as the subway nears Shinjuku?

Waves like hair blowing
As wind lifts and lets go,
This hypnotic rhythm,
Deep and dangerous,
Draws us in and down,
Its ugly beauty blue,
Its weight alive.

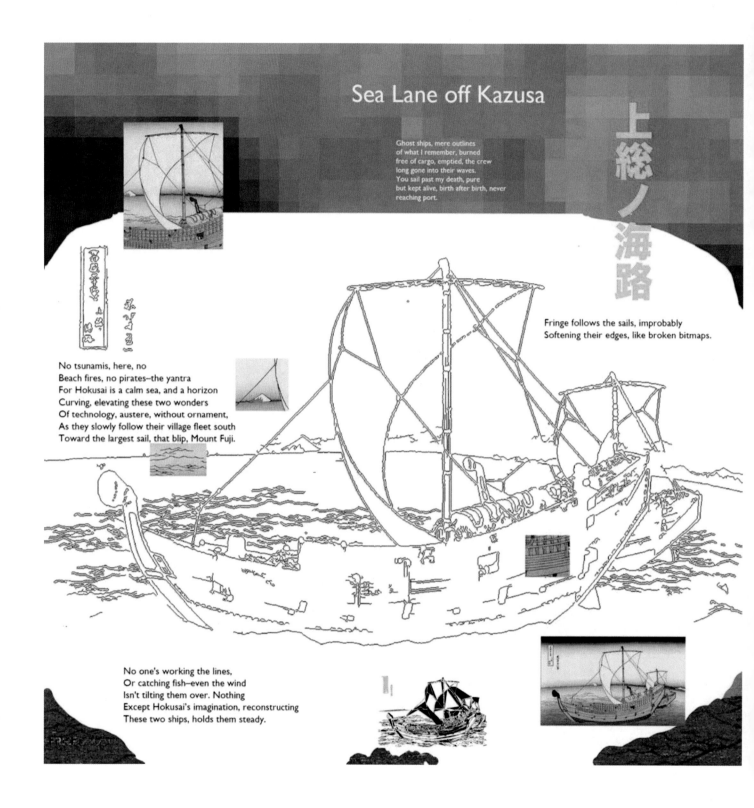

Sea Lane off Kazusa

上総ノ海路

Ghost ships, mere outlines
of what I remember, burned
free of cargo, emptied, the crew
long gone into their waves.
You sail past my death, pure
but kept alive, birth after birth, never
reaching port.

Fringe follows the sails, improbably
Softening their edges, like broken bitmaps.

No tsunamis, here, no
Beach fires, no pirates—the yantra
For Hokusai is a calm sea, and a horizon
Curving, elevating these two wonders
Of technology, austere, without ornament,
As they slowly follow their village fleet south
Toward the largest sail, that blip, Mount Fuji.

No one's working the lines,
Or catching fish—even the wind
Isn't tilting them over. Nothing
Except Hokusai's imagination, reconstructing
These two ships, holds them steady.

Off
Tago
Beach

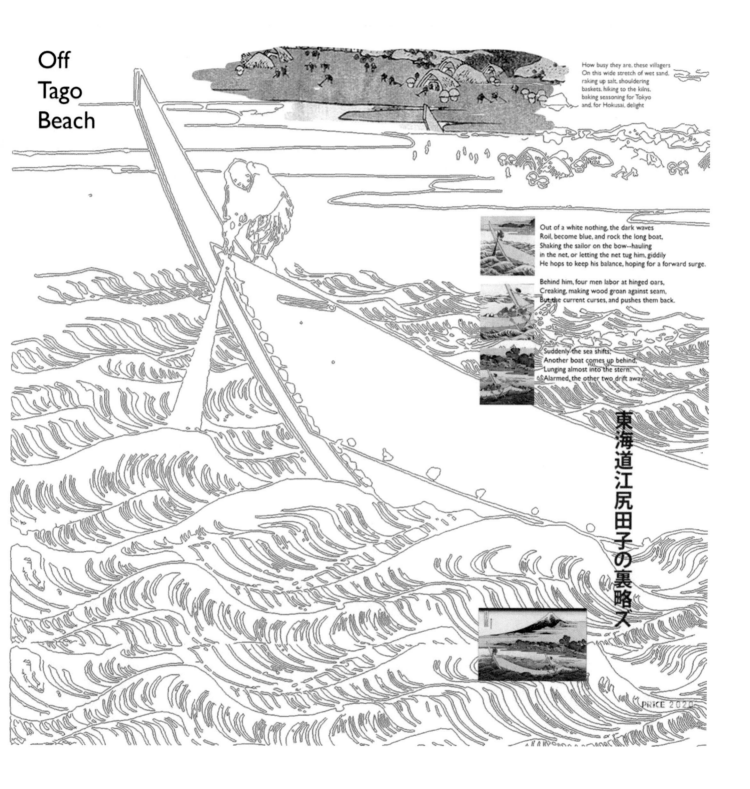

How busy they are, these villagers
On this wide stretch of wet sand,
raking up salt, shouldering
baskets, hiking to the kilns,
baking seasoning for Tokyo
and, for Hokusai, delight

Out of a white nothing, the dark waves
Roil, become blue, and rock the long boat,
Shaking the sailor on the bow--hauling
in the net, or letting the net tug him, giddily
He hops to keep his balance, hoping for a forward surge.

Behind him, four men labor at hinged oars,
Creaking, making wood groan against seam,
But the current curses, and pushes them back.

Suddenly the sea shifts,
Another boat comes up behind,
Lunging almost into the stern.
Alarmed, the other two drift away

東海道江尻田子の裏略ズ

PRICE 2024

Tsukada-jima in Musashi Province

武陽佃島

They are all dead now, these
fishermen, sailors, and villagers,
the trees, too, have been erased,
and the masts against a horizon
no longer green. The immortality
that print asserts is
useless to these souls.

This forested arm slices across the water,
All the way down the coast, to those tiny masts,
Busy about the fish at the curve of the earth,
Drinking the waters melting off the slopes
Of the thawing, but still snowbound Mount Fuji.

Like utopia, the island
floats above the dark waters,
not yet awakened by
first light, waiting for
the morning breeze to slap ropes,
and fill out loose sails.

This big boat, loaded to near sinking, gets
Poled away from the island
as one sailor balances
on the gunnel, trailing
a catch in the wave splash.

On the Coast of Noboto

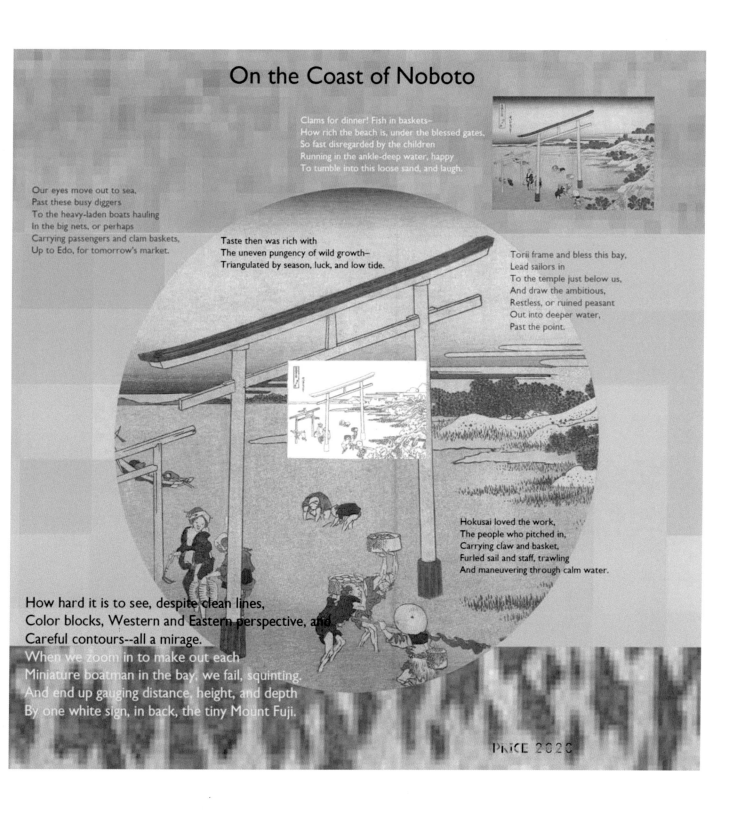

Clams for dinner! Fish in baskets—
How rich the beach is, under the blessed gates.
So fast disregarded by the children
Running in the ankle-deep water, happy
To tumble into this loose sand, and laugh.

Our eyes move out to sea,
Past these busy diggers
To the heavy-laden boats hauling
In the big nets, or perhaps
Carrying passengers and clam baskets,
Up to Edo, for tomorrow's market.

Taste then was rich with
The uneven pungency of wild growth—
Triangulated by season, luck, and low tide.

Torii frame and bless this bay,
Lead sailors in
To the temple just below us,
And draw the ambitious,
Restless, or ruined peasant
Out into deeper water,
Past the point.

Hokusai loved the work,
The people who pitched in,
Carrying claw and basket,
Furled sail and staff, trawling
And maneuvering through calm water.

How hard it is to see, despite clean lines,
Color blocks, Western and Eastern perspective, and
Careful contours--all a mirage.
When we zoom in to make out each
Miniature boatman in the bay, we fail, squinting,
And end up gauging distance, height, and depth
By one white sign, in back, the tiny Mount Fuji.

PRICE 2020

23

Fujimigahara in Owari

Print fades, revives, returns,
going from yellow to beige, bland and back,
editions giving out, ideas circling through.

How slight the almost unnoticed extra,
The modest exclamation, the "over there"
Just poking up, a bit off-center,
The snowpile in summer, his own Mount Fuji!

Muscling the last board tight, Hokusai
Exposes structure, tools, and sweat—
Barrel, or tub, this circle leads us in,
Then we spin, board by board, and pop out
Onto the sand, and some unseen slope
So big it puts us hundreds of feet above
The mudlines between rice paddies;
Pulling back, we conclude we're on a cliff,
Liable to roll off, but no, now
We are inside a tunnel,
Peering through, attention setting in
Perpetual migration,
Around, and in.

Like a taiko drum, this vast O
Bangs on our attention. The periphery
Fades away, one tree becoming a far-off
Forest; the scene is inside the wheel, and out.

PRICE 2019

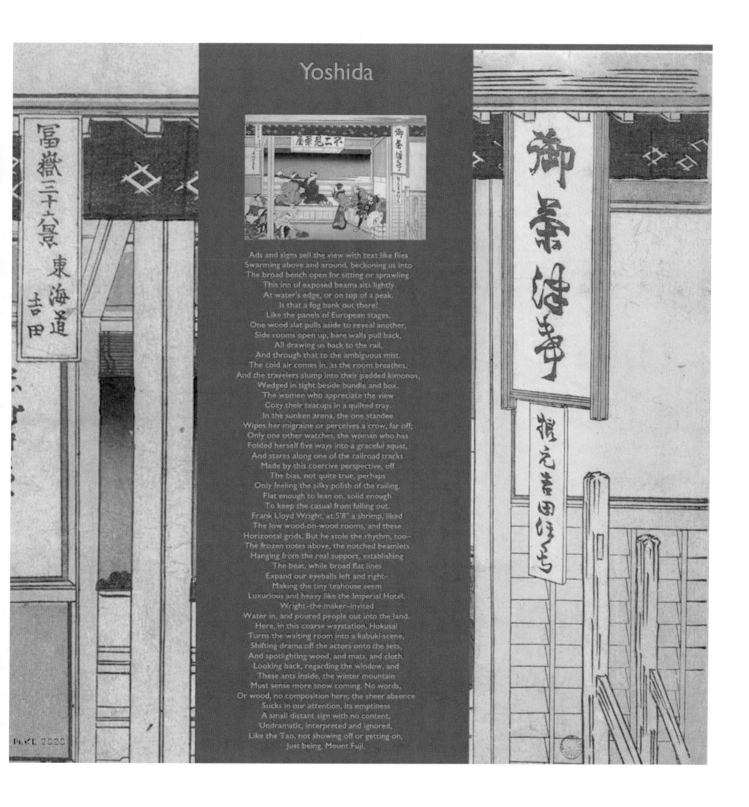

Yoshida

Ads and signs sell the view with text like flies
Swarming above and around, beckoning us into
The broad bench open for sitting or sprawling.
This inn of exposed beams sits lightly
At water's edge, or on top of a peak.
Is that a fog bank out there?
Like the panels of European stages,
One wood slat pulls aside to reveal another,
Side rooms open up, bare walls pull back,
All drawing us back to the rail,
And through that to the ambiguous mist.
The cold air comes in, as the room breathes,
And the travelers slump into their padded kimonos,
Wedged in tight beside bundle and box.
The women who appreciate the view
Cozy their teacups in a quilted tray.
In the sunken arena, the one standee
Wipes her migraine or perceives a crow, far off;
Only one other watches, the woman who has
Folded herself five ways into a graceful squat,
And stares along one of the railroad tracks
Made by this coercive perspective, off
The bias, not quite true, perhaps
Only feeling the silky polish of the railing,
Flat enough to lean on, solid enough
To keep the casual from falling out.
Frank Lloyd Wright, at 5'8" a shrimp, liked
The low wood-on-wood rooms, and these
Horizontal grids. But he stole the rhythm, too—
The frozen notes above, the notched beamlets
Hanging from the real support, establishing
The beat, while broad flat lines
Expand our eyeballs left and right—
Making the tiny teahouse seem
Luxurious and heavy like the Imperial Hotel,
Wright—the maker—invited
Water in, and poured people out into the land.
Here, in this coarse waystation, Hokusai
Turns the waiting room into a kabuki scene,
Shifting drama off the actors onto the sets,
And spotlighting wood, and mats, and cloth.
Looking back, regarding the window, and
These ants inside, the winter mountain
Must sense more snow coming. No words,
Or wood, no composition here; the sheer absence
Sucks in our attention, its emptiness
A small distant sign with no content,
Undramatic, interpreted and ignored,
Like the Tao, not showing off or getting on,
Just being, Mount Fuji.

Sazai Hall, Temple of the 500 Arhats

A network of wooden marvels, worshipped as a temple each slat delineated with love, and good luck carved into the pedestal, like one bell hanging off the eaves.

Isolated above the water, the wood
Creaks and rejoins, its soft surface
Responding to the slippers and heels
As the crowd presses up to the rail,
Unable to hold back, one man crying out,
Pointing, the two women resting at last
On the smooth round railing, looking out
Past the pond, along with the aristocrat,
The man with the itchy scalp, and the girl
Resting next to her huge pack.
Only the little boy ignores it, clinging
To the clump of herbs, resisting all this adult
Hoopla, drawn forward anyway, by his mother,
To make this moment a souvenir, focused
By the landscape on the point
Between two villages,
That magnificent bump, Mount Fuji.

And where now are the tombs
of these unremembered
admirers, and
the kimonos that were so fresh?

Where now is the snow, and the
clean sanded beam?
Wood, water, and wonder
arrange his attention,
architecting the long view,
imprinting this false image, at once
alive with busy visitors, and gone.

PRICE 2020

The Watermill at Onden

How much like rocks these frozen waves
Churned out by the mill owner's wheel,
Tumbling water in its wooden troughs,
Tilting, letting more spill out, like hair,
Then, settling down to the channel, pouring
Everything downstream, the mill roof thatched oddly
To keep rain off the grinding stone, and grain,
Hauled by those men struggling up the path,
Just behind the women gathering water in buckets,
And the curious boy, staring at this chaos
That never ends, just goes on foaming,
And tumbling, and hissing, as his turtle
Tugs, to get away. How calm, now, against this work,
The distant snows of Mount Fuji.

遠江山中

In the Mountains of Tōtōmi

How Hokusai loves wood: he saws planks
Every night, dreams he is fastening beam
And joist and roofbeam with wooden pegs, lashing
Rushes, bamboo, and willow to the shelter.
His architectural imagination lets him construct
Window, rail, porch, bridge and barrel,
Like Pythagoras or Euclid, visualizing
What you can do with a straight line, an angle,
And the pure circle. Here in Tōtōmi
He found the raw scaffolding, roped
To the crimmed trunk, he saw how many hours
It took one man to saw straight down,
Ten fifteen or more feet, not drifting into
The saw track of the man below, sawing up.

Always meditating geometry, Hokusai
Makes triangle upon pyramid, looking
Out at the ideal cone, perfectly placed,
Not centered, because he never liked
To balance; he went as far out,
Cantilevered, as he could, given the weight
And vector of his wood.

Beyond smoke and sweat
The stable form stares,
Not made, but poured, bubbled up,
Then hardened to rock.
From the muscular push and pull, and slant
Force of wood, Hokusai retreats to
The unruffled, the unborn
Mount Fuji.

PRICE

Tatekawa in Honjo

Wood and water—what a scene of industry.
Piled, stacked, tossed, sawed, leaned, and loaded.
This wood's becoming modular, and the long strips
Stand vertically waiting for the air to cure, destined
For a daimyo's reception hall, or a temple repair.
When Toshi's father visited the twenty-six temples
His ancestors had built, every priest wrote
Asking for money to repair the roof, the statue,
The floor or steps. This lumberyard's an act
Of worship, too, reaching skyward, hugging
The inlet, ready to ship beams, heavy or light,
All the way to Tokyo, from this compound, where
Thatch makes an instant roof over piles so tall
An American would topple. The precision of these saws
Echoes Hokusai's own: he must have loved cutting those
Straight lines into the wooden tablet, imitating
The tight grain, creating so many flat surfaces
With so many intervening slants and slopes
We see depth where there is no tone, accept
The outline for gradations, and enjoy its pure
Reproducibility. Nothing seems fuzzy here.
Even the horizon blue—is that the sea?—lives distinctly.
He's also saying how hard the hewers and sawyers
Must have worked, just as he did, to make a series of cuts.
Build and unbuild these towers like a distillate
Of the forest outside of town. Seeing through wood
Not clothes, Hokusai's answer to Anne Hollander:
He makes us struggle to unveil, undress, get through,
Like a male brushing aside the petticoats, to glimpse
The delicately withdrawn, modestly quiet Mount Fuji.

Honganji Temple at Asakusa

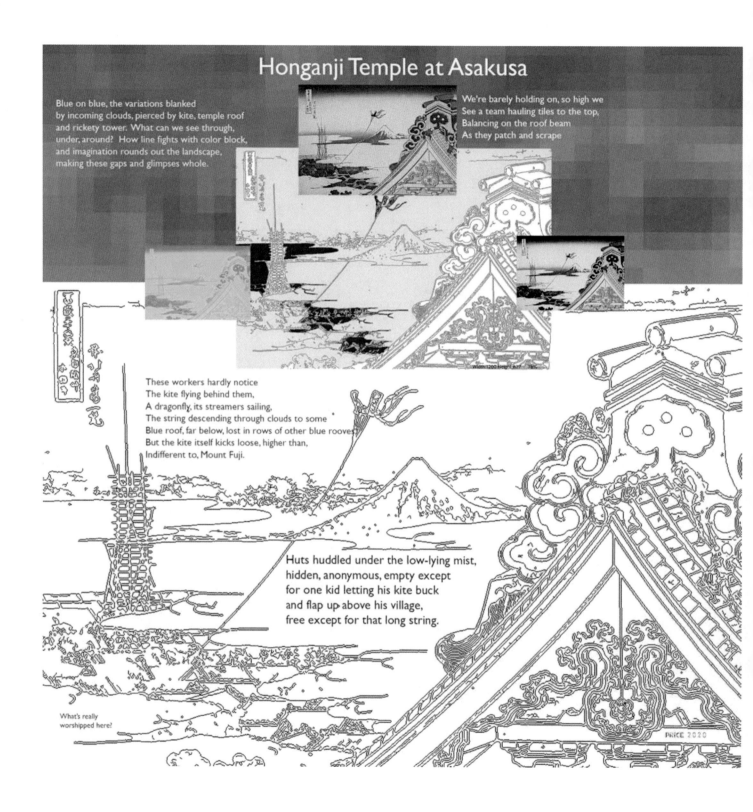

Blue on blue, the variations blanked
by incoming clouds, pierced by kite, temple roof
and rickety tower. What can we see through,
under, around? How line fights with color block,
and imagination rounds out the landscape,
making these gaps and glimpses whole.

We're barely holding on, so high we
See a team hauling tiles to the top,
Balancing on the roof beam
As they patch and scrape

These workers hardly notice
The kite flying behind them,
A dragonfly, its streamers sailing,
The string descending through clouds to some
Blue roof, far below, lost in rows of other blue rooves
But the kite itself kicks loose, higher than,
Indifferent to, Mount Fuji.

Huts huddled under the low-lying mist,
hidden, anonymous, empty except
for one kid letting his kite buck
and flap up above his village,
free except for that long string.

What's really
worshipped here?

PRICE 2020

Mitsui Shop at Suruga-chō in Edo

These workers at the peak tossing rope and thatch,
Can barely hang onto these gray tiles.
One man balancing on his big toe, arms waving,
Too far from the ladder to go down,
Too skewed to flatten on the roof; in-between,
He pivots, like Hokusai, so adroit up front,
But a little iffy in the hips.

Work builds
the architecture of the scene,
setting off the slats, the tiles,
the triangular roof with
earthbound, sweaty, precarious
men who ignore the kites sailing
above and beyond, their paper frames
clattering on the shiftless breeze.

江都駿河町三井見世略図

We read the inn signs,
And our eye is led back to a white sea,
Expecting equal clarity, and not quite finding the fact,
Revising the vista, rising
Up the colorless snows of Mount Fuji.

PRICE 2020

Out of the narrow seaside neighborhood they come,
Burdened and backpacked, struggling up this arching bridge,
So steep they have to lean into every step, climbing
Toward the teetering top, where two men rest,
Watching the traders pole their boat free.

We pierce the bridge, looking
for Mount Fuji, so obscure
it seems a cloud, or a mistake.

Examined
Up close, the lines
Become abstract. But
Pull back, and hue
Suffuses shore
And bridge as
Symmetry
Controls the crowd
By such magic,
Hokusai
Imprisons and awakes
A trembling white breeze.

Moss slithers down this wall,
Followed by ivy, rock after
Rock, impenetrable.

Under the Mannen Bridge at Fukagawa

So uncomfortably perched on these rocks,
Intent on fish, he ignores bridge, boats & view.

PRICE
2020

Nihonbashi

How European this perfect V,
leading our eye back
past wharf and warehouse—
fish and flat and skiff—
into the Imperial palace,
its stones big as huts,
transforming our perspective,
blurred by clouds or snow,
its one sharp point,
off center
the colorless icon,
a Japanese character,
Mount Fuji.

Printing fills
his black contours
with hue and shade,
leaving sky untouched,
the original medium

One wise boatman
Poles away, past these
fish-stinking loading docks

In the foreground
the bridge
bulges
with hats, bags,
bundles and
carts, spilling
these people
out of frame
into our lap

Men like flecks of foam,
Waves like well-combed hair,
And colors crisp as dawn—
Small sparks arousing a plethora.

Neutral as a soul,
Hokusai shifts focus from this churn
To the image of a sound
These travelers cannot hear—
Calm Mount Fuji,
The background hum.

We're back on the road, without Jack Kerouac,
Where the highway fords the rough water, & every aristocrat
Gets to ride his porter's shoulders. The bearers barely
Keep nose above foam, as their big boxes and bales
Risk squashing them, and sinking, right,
In the middle of the crossing. Current laps at
The poles, little rocks threaten the balance
Of the porters, with their clumsy shifting human loads.
Why not go around? The opening in the sand dunes,
And the main street of town leads right to this passage.
But what's over on our right, where the tide seems to have left,
And how can there be such waves, and such depth so fast?
Like a tsunami, overwhelming a beachfront street,
Or the sudden tide that overtook King John
And his baggage, struggling in wet sand.
This water's no friend. The teams could be competing
In a festival, but no one stands on the shore to applaud,
Or laugh, seeing the lead man on the green box go down,
Clawing at the smooth front, but not helped,
Because his neighbors need both arms to hold the poles.

Crossing the Ōi River at Kanaya on the Tōkaidō Highway

Shichiri Beach in Sagami

Prints vary by age, paper, carver and Impression. What stays solid, unmoved, as our eyes search for boat, smoke, or sign of life?

So hard to see, despite clean lines and empty space, Hokusai tempts us to imagine, deep within his landscape, the ripple, the fall and the receding wave

Inside the third hut she boils snow for tea,
Pulling tight the padded winter kimono,
Running her free hand over the coals.
Wind lifts up through the floorboards,
Ruffling the double tatami.
They ate the last fish yesterday,
And the boat's still not fixed.

Flecking the surface with quick slashes
He makes a dozen waves emerge
from the frozen bay.

Up on the hill, his toes clenching,
Hokusai sees underneath the thatch
To the wooden dipper she uses,
And the black pot. He knows
The silence that snow imposes—
Leveling the beach, making the road
Impassable, beyond the islands.

The sea's
A blank.

PRICE 2020

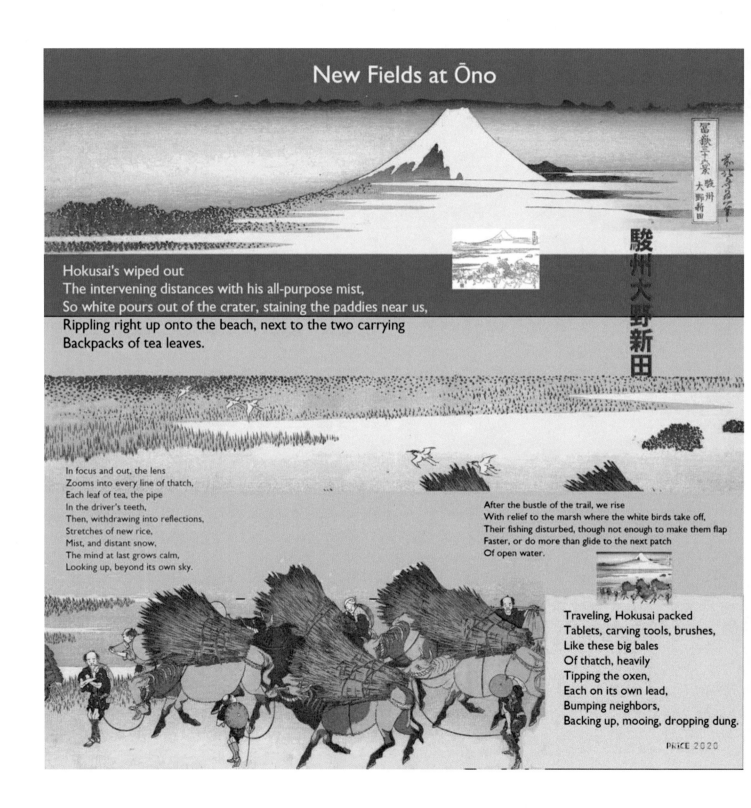

New Fields at Ōno

冨嶽三十六景
駿州
大野新田

駿州大野新田

Hokusai's wiped out
The intervening distances with his all-purpose mist,
So white pours out of the crater, staining the paddies near us,
Rippling right up onto the beach, next to the two carrying
Backpacks of tea leaves.

In focus and out, the lens
Zooms into every line of thatch,
Each leaf of tea, the pipe
In the driver's teeth,
Then, withdrawing into reflections,
Stretches of new rice,
Mist, and distant snow,
The mind at last grows calm,
Looking up, beyond its own sky.

After the bustle of the trail, we rise
With relief to the marsh where the white birds take off,
Their fishing disturbed, though not enough to make them flap
Faster, or do more than glide to the next patch
Of open water.

Traveling, Hokusai packed
Tablets, carving tools, brushes,
Like these big bales
Of thatch, heavily
Tipping the oxen,
Each on its own lead,
Bumping neighbors,
Backing up, mooing, dropping dung.

PRICE 2020

Hills at Gotenyama
above Shinagawa

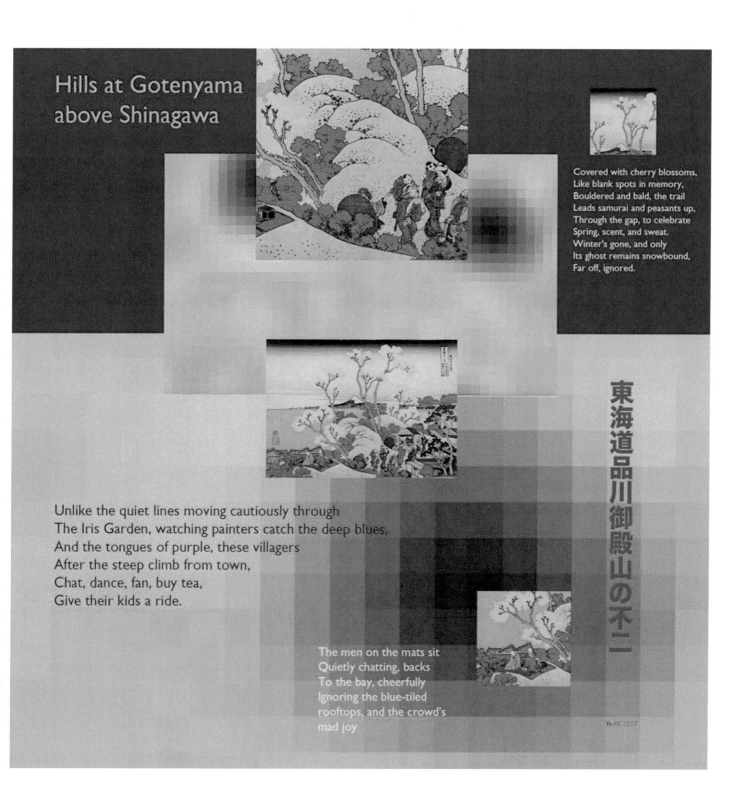

Covered with cherry blossoms,
Like blank spots in memory,
Bouldered and bald, the trail
Leads samurai and peasants up,
Through the gap, to celebrate
Spring, scent, and sweat.
Winter's gone, and only
Its ghost remains snowbound,
Far off, ignored.

Unlike the quiet lines moving cautiously through
The Iris Garden, watching painters catch the deep blues,
And the tongues of purple, these villagers
After the steep climb from town,
Chat, dance, fan, buy tea,
Give their kids a ride.

The men on the mats sit
Quietly chatting, backs
To the bay, cheerfully
Ignoring the blue-tiled
rooftops, and the crowd's
mad joy

東海道品川御殿山の不二

The Lake at Hakone in Sagami

To wake up mid-dream, to catch
Hokusai alive within the mirage,
We press in, zooming to see, what?
Empty space, blank time, drops
Of pigment, slices in wood.

The blue rooves
Whisper together, hunkered down
So low their owners can't see more than the tip,
Or sense the presence,
Behind these flat fog fingers,
Of that freezing eye,
The austere ghost, Mount Fuji.

Without people we long for houses,
And discover three nested in the rocks;
What happened to the underbrush?
Are we so high that shrubs can't grow?
Or have these peasants stripped the shore,
Mowed the hill, to live?

相州箱根湖水

PRICE 2020

Misaka in Kai

The morning sky bleaches the rock slides,
stubbly as an old man's chin, the three slopes
that catch snow in winter, and in Hokusai's
upside-down reflection, the after-image,
the blueprint of Mount Fuji.

Two stories high, these
thatched hipgon spikes that
rhyme with the mountaintop, huddle
their little triangles underneath
the softly curving
and bumpy, irregular hills.

甲州三坂水面

Telescoping what we can see from the other side,
Hokusai zooms us into an unnaturally large boat,
poling toward the confluence, undisturbed by wave
or breeze, a momentary marker of work,
that fisherman perhaps, the only soul awake.

How neat the ghost, the inverted, wait, no,
the mountain on the water is, well,
snowcapped, not the drab beige peak we see
above Lake Kawaguchi. Or are these blue streaks
just hints of sediment sluicing downstream,
staining the inlet, going from grey to light blue to dark,
losing their burden as they sink into the silent lake?

PRICE 2020

Kajikazawa in Kai Province

How far from the live image this print
Imagines storm and calm, cloud reach,
Five cormorants on their leashes, under the water,
An experience echoed but not revived,
Caught off-balance, and gone.

How like a gentle breast,
Emerging whitely from a silken blouse,
Its nipple irregular, aroused, off center,
As if waiting for the tongue to touch down,
Or teeth to nip, as the whole body,
Delicately veiled, rises into tension,
White sea, white sky, pouring down
But not quite reaching our chaotic hearts,
So far from the divine love, so ignorant
Of our own Mount Fuji.

The boy sorts fish,
Huddled like a barnacle, braced against
The violent wind, the tons of thrashing foam,
And the thump of weighted water.

Lava so sharp its cuts never heal,
Waves like carved coral, the froth
Rising from deep impulses—no beach here.

Each print a different hue, indigo,
green, or orange, impressing itself on
wood, repeating wave after wave,
each the same, each unique.

PRICE 2019

Nakahara in Sagami

He did not scorn a little artifice,
Setting up these caricatures
Like actors on the road, too big
For their places in perspective,
And he had no shame in setting
A crowd at the crossroads,
When one or two, at most, appeared.

How he loved investigating
Treasures wrapped in cloth
Tucked in a box,
Rolled up in an umbrella,
Or nested inside the white slope.

The commemorative stone
Has been eaten away by weather or war,
And the chimes hanging from the ropes look
As if they've lost a few pieces.
For Hokusai, time cannot be
Contained, but compressed,
Seven moments in one view,
Captured almost alive.

I love these little bridges like those in Kyoto
Across the ditches and canals, too narrow
For two to pass, at least with boxes hanging
From your shoulder or hoe in hand.

PRICE 2020

41

Jonathan Reeve Price

The Inume Pass in Kai Province

With each new impression, the nearby hill
grows green or blue, and, farther off,
Mount Fuji's slopes turn brown,
or fade to red.
But at the top, in print after print,
snow remains without a hue,
a sharp nothing.

Distance acts as an excuse
For making each layer separate, except where
These two trees just accidentally
Intervene

Even these ridge-climbers cannot see
The water below, as they pick
A solid path up, past
The steep ravine.

Data dropout? Or pixels with no clue?
A heavy mist sets in, or ground fog–
Between us and it, a mile or two of steam
From the lake or gorge below.

Walruslike, the small hills
Unfold ahead, rising.

These tiny traders are too tired to care,
Tugging their horses, they
Just keep going.
No sightseeing here. Just work.

PRICE 2020

Shimo Meguro

How slowly I drink my tea,
Tasting the bitter earth inside,
Direct from the field.

The bald man picks
Each tea leaf out of the nearby field
In Kyoto, I saw men
Climb narrow triangles—
Bamboo ladders—
And snip each dead needle off a pine,
Packing their finds carefully into bags.

Row after row, the tea makes topographic lines,
Blocking erosion, forcing the worker to tiptoe
Leaning into the slope, carrying his hoe and lunch.

Look! In the bullet train, these hills of tea go by,
Steep, sharp, small, family-size, raked and terraced,
So overworked it's amazing the plants yield leaves.

Tea Fields at Katakura in Suruga

A process diagram, showing tea flowing from field to hand to back and onto horses, and into storage, Hokusai's image is lean, but agile, complexity nested in wisps of fog, as the unpredictable behavior, art, emerges, like Mount Fuji, unmelted on this spring day.

駿州片倉茶園の不二

Like a thousand reeds forming thatch, or a million small leaves becoming tea, the village turns out as one, a hundred-handed hive, singing.

Sitting together at the bench, breathing in the first flush of flowers, plucking leaves as small as one joint of my finger, we fill our barrels, we chat, we make men carry, dry, and store our economy, green tea, ready to go to Tokyo. No ceremony here, just the rhythm of pick, drop, prune, and taste our gentle, unwilted, still pungent communal crop, our trade for rice.

Sky, sky, sky–like the shogun economy
A dead hand. But underneath, the people
Clamber along, carrying turnips. Trade
Climbs out of the shallows, unnoticed
By this enormous atmosphere, stretching
To the dark blue of outer space, marked only
By that other island, the pure one,
The inhuman Mount Fuji.

Sōshū Enoshima

Like teeth revealed by receding gums, the town
Rises above the beach, built on lava walls,
Barricaded against the piles of loose sand.
Past the twin towers, the travelers go in,
Down a street we see only in the rooves,
Headed uphill to the 6-layered temple,
Or perhaps out to the point, to rest.

From the surface, we guess the snug,
Tree-pressed small town life, so much like
West Newbury. My great-great-grandfather
Docked here, on his black ship,
Shopped for boxes, maps, and fans,
And brought them back to the cold, dark farm
In Massachusetts. But no Hokusai
Sat on the far bank, sketching the Merrimack.
Only Thoreau paddled by,
And the peddler painters, who would put
Your face in a pre-drawn body,
Then leave before it dried. In these artifacts,
I still smell the fish, and the balls of rice.

Perspective, still geometric for Hokusai,
Delicately suggested by so many straight lines,
Gives way to a green panorama,
Each blotch a clump of leaves, or wave,
Dwarfing that irregular line of ants,
This one with a cane,
That one with a blanket on its back.

Smudges, the men and horses advance
Across the sandspit, briefly cleared
By the withdrawing tide–so small
The scrambling legs of a horse and rider
Look like a flea with a hat on.

Artificial as a stage curtain, fingers
Of fog spread over the shoals, obscuring
Spars, tufted islands, the facts
That would let us gauge the width,
Length, and solidity of this sudden path.

45

Surugadai in Edo

Carrying a bag of leaves as big as he is,
The gardener staggers up the yellow hill,
Another man, bent over with his wicker backpack,
Points out one leaf he missed; the lord inspects,
Halting his three shaved-head porters on the slope,
across the steps from the lean-to cook shack,
and the farmers returning from market, backs loaded—
all this bustle up and down, past these huge earthworks,
the palace grounds, the great ditch,
and the puffs of green, the trees wobbling up
into a pure beige sky, higher than these rooves,
so diagonally adroit, slicing the foreground,
and, on the horizon, the simple shape that all lines point to
little Mount Fuji.

The tan fisherman blocks out
our view of the blue stream.
Then dark trees obscure
the slope, that hides
the lava wall inserted
between us and some trees,
and these treetops
mask waves of houses that stumble,
roof after roof,
toward the mountain they approach,
but cannot surround, or top,
the whole scene
cut off
by a gigantic house behind
yes, more landscape.

How adroitly Hokusai
creates depth.

Through such interruptions Hokusai
leads us back, teasing the eye
to retrace these meandering paths
past highway, house, and
baskets of tea leaves
to a single point.

Senju in Musashi Province

Repeated forms deceive
The rapid mind, so
Eager to dismiss.
Only the quiet eye
Can lose itself
In these slow and small
Distractions, the thatch
Of a pleasure house,
And rest after a long march.

Against the sameness of the houses on the far side,
And the flatness of the in-reach of the bay,
The men are out of order, headed every which way.
Taking their red tubes to many directions that
I recall deliberate randomness, numbers chosen
Because they form no order we can recognize.

The archers I saw in the subway headed for the competition carried
Red tubes like these. A little short for the long curve of a bow,
Too light for a broad sword, these tubes look menacing.
Are those short blades at their waists?
Why so many in uniform?
Trouble trundling through the village,
And the two women out on the trail
Sit down to watch, perhaps hoping to be able to say,
We saw it all, from the beach path.

Left foot, right foot, shoulder
Pitched and turned, the soldiers
Form a line, yes, but each makes
His own saunter, slouch, or stare.

The Fields of Umezawa in Sagami

What started all blue, azure, and faded hues,
Becomes full color, the red crests popping
From each crane, and the hills now green.
What remains blue—the puddle and the volcano,
Plus an indeterminate ground, arbitrarily deep.
Hokusai's fluid line allows fresh ink
To pour bright life into the void we read as fog.

Delighted, the cranes drink, preen, and call—
The couple sails off for the hill that's been
Logged so thoroughly it looks like chin stubble,
Or perhaps to the slope where trees do survive
Far up the summer slope of the landmark
We all spot from the Japan Airlines windows,
As we stuff our inflight magazine into
The seatback silkscreened with another crane in a circle,
And every Japanese says how pretty,
In the tone Californians use for Tuolomne meadows
Or Yosemite, that dying swoon,
The pleasure of at last seeing the original of
The TV emblem, or red neon ad,
Guaranteeing all some inner grace, like the touch
Of temple smoke on the forehead,
Good fortune brushed in priestly calligraphy,
Or a photo souvenir, capturing
The sentiment and the corporate mark, Mount Fuji.

A Fine, Breezy Day

The clouds ride by, regular as furrows.

93 houses he had, 50 false names, dozens
Of bankruptcies—wood carver,
Errand boy, calendar-seller, pepper salesman.
At 60 he knuckled down to art.
At 78, burned out of his house, he shrugged,
And rebuilt, with a sign warning visitors,
"No compliments. No gifts."

Who but a madman would plunk
This simple triangle, this solid block
of undifferentiated color at the subtle heart
of so many prints?
No fake crags, no Chinese mist,
just a big bald mountain
that he makes his own.

The forest creeps up the slope,
a green blur, with treetops, or shadows
suggesting depth, or pines, or, really, sharp cuts
in the wood, from Hokusai's black slashes
hacking away at the smooth flat block.

How I love Hokusai, the mirror-polisher who painted
Buddha big enough to eat a horse, impromptu,
Then switched brushes, and sketched two sparrows,
So tiny you needed a magnifying glass to see.
Expressionist, he threw a paper door down,
dipped a rooster's five-clawed feet in red ink,
And set him running—making
Maple Leaves in Autumn.

Red lava burns up the cone
Melts the last snow, soars up past
These low, encircling trees.

How many colors fade and pop, as publishers
print indigo, Prussian blue, red and green,
each edition improvising, adding
life to lava, each press making its own air
almost visible.

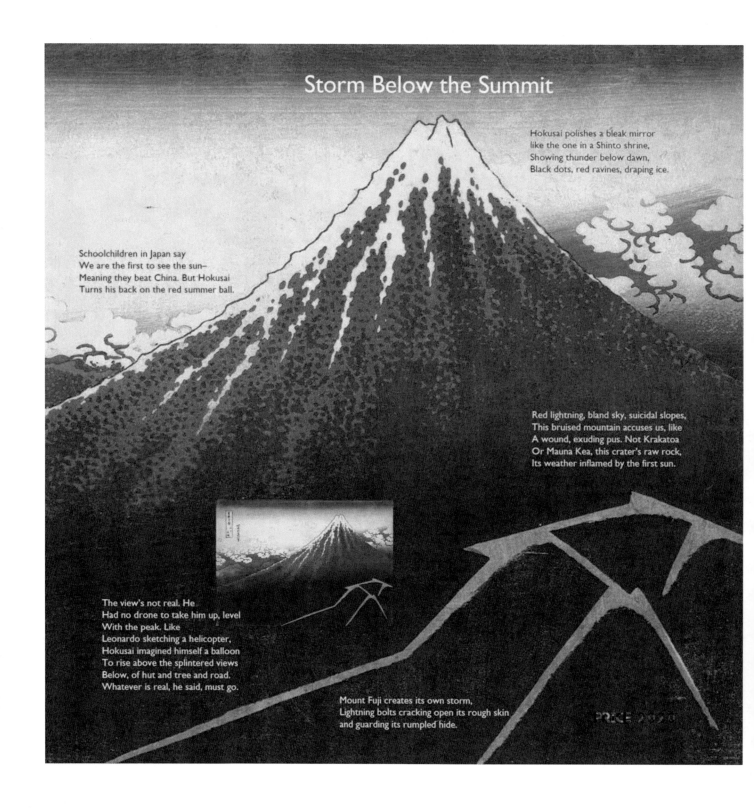

Storm Below the Summit

Hokusai polishes a bleak mirror
like the one in a Shinto shrine,
Showing thunder below dawn,
Black dots, red ravines, draping ice.

Schoolchildren in Japan say
We are the first to see the sun—
Meaning they beat China. But Hokusai
Turns his back on the red summer ball.

Red lightning, bland sky, suicidal slopes,
This bruised mountain accuses us, like
A wound, exuding pus. Not Krakatoa
Or Mauna Kea, this crater's raw rock,
Its weather inflamed by the first sun.

The view's not real. He
Had no drone to take him up, level
With the peak. Like
Leonardo sketching a helicopter,
Hokusai imagined himself a balloon
To rise above the splintered views
Below, of hut and tree and road.
Whatever is real, he said, must go.

Mount Fuji creates its own storm,
Lightning bolts cracking open its rough skin
and guarding its rumpled hide.

PRICE 2020

Dawn at Isawa in Kai Province

These fogbanks softly slice across
The middle world, leaving us unsure
If water is air, or if these stripes are
Shadows, low hills, or holes puncturing
Cloud cover, mist, or empty air.

Lines Xray
What colors
Blur.

First light lifts water and rooftops,
Leaving people dim--we spot their hats,
As they straggle out of the inn
But the dawn hides their faces
as they load horses, lift boxes,
stretch, and start the trail.

The Other Side of Mt. Fuji, from the Minobu River

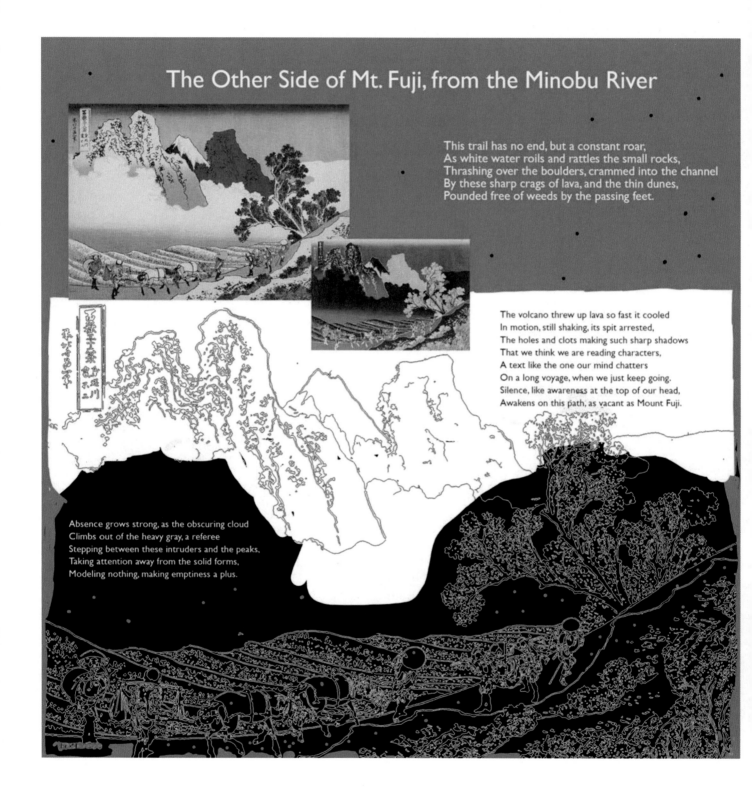

This trail has no end, but a constant roar,
As white water roils and rattles the small rocks,
Thrashing over the boulders, crammed into the channel
By these sharp crags of lava, and the thin dunes,
Pounded free of weeds by the passing feet.

The volcano threw up lava so fast it cooled
In motion, still shaking, its spit arrested,
The holes and clots making such sharp shadows
That we think we are reading characters,
A text like the one our mind chatters
On a long voyage, when we just keep going.
Silence, like awareness at the top of our head,
Awakens on this path, as vacant as Mount Fuji.

Absence grows strong, as the obscuring cloud
Climbs out of the heavy gray, a referee
Stepping between these intruders and the peaks,
Taking attention away from the solid forms,
Modeling nothing, making emptiness a plus.

Climbing Mt. Fuji

And now Mount Fuji's gone,
Or the image of its crater in the distance,
Because we're on it, for the first time,
Looking at the cave of the ancestors,
Clambering over the erratic lava,
Up the ladders, and along the trail we've chosen.
Is this the inner shrine?
Do the thousand and one Buddhas
Bless those who have come so far,
And bowed? We see now how like water
The lava is, even after hardening;
Dangerous, but put on pause,
On some August day before the snows return,
Cutting off the passes, and killing
Anyone who comes too late, or stays too long.

He whittles each woodblock like a walking stick,
To move beyond. Imagination
Serves to magnify, not trap, the energy he uses
To surround, invade, and then abandon
People, horses, hats, trees, and self.
What's left? His soul, a polished mirror,
Reflects its source, by envisioning,
Then leaving to the divine, Mount Fuji.

Afterword

Now that I am 79, I like contemplating images and texts created by other old folks, like Hokusai. When he celebrated his 75th birthday, Hokusai wrote:

From the age of six I had a penchant for copying the form of things, and from about fifty, my pictures were frequently published; but until the age of seventy, nothing that I drew was worthy of notice.

At seventy- three years, I was able to fathom the growth of plants and trees, and the structure of birds, animals, insects and fish.

Thus when I reach eighty years, I hope to have made increasing progress, and at ninety to see further into the underlying principles of things, so that at one hundred years I will have achieved a divine state in my art, and at one hundred and ten, every dot and every stroke will seem as though alive.

Those of you who live long enough, bear witness that these words of mine prove not false.
Told by Gakyō _Rōjin Manji

Translated by Henry Smith, in *Hokusai: One Hundred Views of Mount Fuji,* Thames and Hudson, London, 1988.

To imitate Hokusai:... When I was 50, I had published more than two dozen books, pioneered online help for Apple, exhibited conceptual art and concrete poetry in New York galleries, and coached almost a thousand professional writers entering the computer field.

One day, having worked with Hiraku Amemiya and Nagatoshi Inagaki in training Japanese technical writers to adjust to the expectations of Western audiences, I took a day off and went to the Tokyo National Museum, in Ueno Park. In Room 10 of the Honkan galleries, I found Hokusai among the "floating world prints" (ukiyo-e) and fashions from the 17th through the 19th century. In that dim space his work jumped off the wall.

Condemned by many critics as not truly representative of Japanese art, his landscapes mix techniques from Dutch copper plate engravings, Chinese paintings, and an eclectic group of design studios in Edo, as Tokyo was known in the 19th century. These cheap commercial prints, available for the price of a bowl of noodles, bursting with vivid blue and white images, spotted with red, green, pink, and grey, outshone the scrolls and fans nearby, which had far more subtle wabi sabi.

Nothing here was meditative, melancholy, simple, or even natural, like the flecks of sumi ink flung off from a brush stroke. These are prints, mechanically reproduced. Instead of showing a single monk on a large scroll, these relatively small pictures are jammed with many people at work. And these are not kabuki actors, or demons, or warriors. Ordinary life, then, caught on the run: these people are mid-stride, turning, climbing, setting fires, sawing wood, stacking lumber, fishing. How alive they seem!

I wanted the whole series. In the gift store, I found a brown linen-bound box of postcards of the entire 36 Views of Mount Fuji, totalling, of course, 46 images. I slipped the ivory stick, unfolded the cord that sealed the lid, and took out the pack—hefty as a set of oversized playing cards.

For months, I sat with the cards, writing poems about each one—a way to explore the images, and to imagine my way into Hokusai's point of view. Where did his attention go? How did he seize on one aspect of the scene, and assemble a cast of characters, showing how they might have all been in motion at one instant?

Hypertext

When I was 60, I published these poems as a hypertext series. What does that mean? At the top of the web page I showed the Hokusai image, and below that, my text, sprinkled with links. Whenever the word *pine* showed up in one poem, for example, I made it into a link to the next poem that mentioned pine trees, and the next.

I was showing verbally the thick interpenetration of the subjects—the repeated themes, you might call them, the subjects that Hokusai kept coming back to, such as bridges, streams, rivers, forests, and of course, Mount Fuji.

This dense thicket of interconnected links was, perhaps, a bit of a formal experiment, driven by my experiences at Apple creating a new form of documentation, now known as online help. We had used HyperCard back then to create procedures and reference panels, each thought of as a separate card, held together with links from menus and highlighted phrases in the content.

Hypertext makes visible the interwoven nature of content. Back when Tim Berners-Lee came up with the HTML vocabulary and the IP protocols, his aim, originally, was to allow researchers to jump from a footnote in one report to the source document. That simple action, clicking and going, is now second nature.

But when we were inventing online help back at Apple, we were wrestling with a new way of conceiving the organization of our material—as a network, not a document. And that was what my series was exploring.

Alas, my experiment put more emphasis on the links than the pictures. And when you clicked, a word, you arrived in the middle of the page, where the next instance of that word appeared, rather than at the top, where you could start reading. The effect was staccato, and unsettling.

Plus, I had not integrated the image and the text. We've now become accustomed to memes where text and icons plop on top of the image, making a comment, or counterpoint—some meaningful mélange. In the past, we thought of art as separate from poetry, complementary, perhaps, or mutually entangled, but still, distinct media. No longer.

With computers we can turn all types of content into electrons, allowing us to mix what used to be distinct media. We build that interpenetration with apps that allow quick videos, short messages, memes. But the designers of museum web sites, art magazines, and critical books stick to the traditional distinction: the reproduction of the artwork stands separate from the text about it.

To me, that separation bangs up against the nature of the tools we are using—the digital data, the algorithmic code, the brilliant hardware, which together define our work environment. As a creator, I am indirectly collaborating with all these software and hardware engineers, and even though I am the "user," their products help me capture, manipulate, integrate, transmit, and publish. How can I not be affected? And why not reflect that collaboration in my final output?

Thinking along these lines, I began to explore these revered images—digitally. I took my cue from Hokusai's own practice.

Zooming

In picture after picture in the series, 36 Views of Mount Fuji, Hokusai invites us to keep zooming in, searching for the little white triangle, the simple shape at the back. So I began by selecting images in the public domain, bringing them up in Photoshop, and magnifying.

The original prints are roughly 10 x 15 inches (25.5 x 37.7 cm), for about 250 square inches of surface. I decided to make my remixes much larger, so I could examine details more closely.

Where Hokusai fitted his drawings into a neat rectangle, with dimensions determined by the wood blocks used in printing, I gave myself more room. In Photoshop, I created a blank canvas 24 x 24 inches (61 x 61 cm), for 1,056 square inches. To me, that square echoes the shape of a picture element (pixel)—the smallest addressable unit within the grid that makes up the monitor screen. Then I enlarged the original image, sometimes by 100% or 200% or more, and slid it around on this canvas, so that only part of the original showed up—the part with Mount Fuji. At other times, I zoomed in even more, to look at the actual pixellation of the colors, when magnified in Preview, captured in a screenshot, and then enlarged some more.

Having zoomed way in, I pulled back to add, on top, a tiny version of the original, for comparison. I wanted to encourage that movement back and forth, that activity, looking first at the blown-up detail, then squinting at the whole it was originally a part of.

Revising

Hokusai often revised his work. We still have some of his first drafts, marked up with red ink, and then the final versions, showing that he was not afraid of completely redoing a drawing—and that he could reproduce much of the first draft in his second— quite a feat, given the intricate mesh of fine lines.

The computer makes this kind of reconsideration, revision, and rethinking much easier for someone like me, even though I have little skill in drawing. So I often moved the thumbnail of the original picture around, on top of the gigantic detail, asking myself: Does it fit there? Does it disrupt our view of the detail? Where does it do the least damage to the section I have selected and enlarged?

Layering

When the block carvers made the key block, the one that outlined all the elements of the picture, they printed a proof for Hokusai.

He marked that up to show them what colors should go where—dark blue at the top, for example, for sky, and light green for distant hills, perhaps.

Then the carvers made a separate block for each color, showing just the areas that required blue, say, or green.

The printer ran the key block first, getting the outlines of shapes down, then ran additional blocks to fill in each color.

Hokusai, then, thought in layers—colors landing on top of outlined shapes, one after another.

In Photoshop, I moved the thumbnail of the original around on one layer, without disturbing anything below it. And I sometimes added other thumbnails, other little details, other views of the original, all sliding around on their own layers, so that none of them erased or damaged anything else.

Because each image lived on its own layer, I was able to make some little images overlap others, suggesting that some recede from us, while others come forward, giving the illusion of depth. I got the idea from Hokusai who suggested fingers of fog between us and Mount Fuji, or inserted a hill half way between us and a beach.

Layers let me build up a complex composition, giving the eye plenty to think about, as it interprets the intervening items, and figures out a path back through this undefined space to Mount Fuji, hiding in the distance.

Imagining Depth

Hokusai, too, draws us into the space of his pictures. At times he adopts the central perspective made popular by Dutch prints, showing, say, two rows of warehouses converging as they go back, getting smaller and smaller until they almost meet—but he interposes a tiny building, to make us imagine, but not see, the vanishing point.

At other times, he puts one element in front of another, in front of another, and so on, exaggerating what the Japanese call near/far (enkin no dosu) …again, giving us the sense that there must be quite a bit of distance between the item in the foreground, and the one in back. Bridges, for instance, stand between us and whatever Hokusai shows us underneath the arch.

Or he inserts huge fingers of fog between us and Mount Fuji, fudging the distance, making it unclear how far away the mountain really is, but making us imagine the intervening geography.

I am not so illusionistic, but I too like to suggest depth. To draw the eye deep into the picture, I sometimes stack items so that some stand in front of others, persuading the mind to imagine moving, step by step, from the foreground to the background, even though the intervening spaces are poorly defined and ambiguous.

Borrowing a technique from the Yamato-e tradition, Hokusai sometimes inserts cloud banks between us and distant hills, making the wet air into distinct, clearly contoured objects. This convention, known as kumogata, is defiantly symbolic, suggesting more than showing, printlike more than painterly, simply blocking our view, but suggesting that there may many miles between us and Mount Fuji, poking up in the back.

For me, a patch of pixels, basically a screenshot of the original picture zoomed way, way in, can serve a similar role for me, creating an uncertain space that echoes the real, but in a way that is clearly abstract, not "realistic."

Colors

At times, as a tribute to the black-and-white drawings that Hokusai submitted to the printers, I bleach all color out of the scene, to demonstrate the fine lines that Hokusai exulted in, challenging the men who had to carve those into the cherry wood blocks for printing.

The pre-publication advertisement for the 36 Views of Mount Fuji stressed that they would be printed in blue ("aizuri ichimai"). And the first five prints were printed entirely in different saturations of the fashionable imported pigment known as Prussian blue, to suggest the dim light of dawn. In the next pictures, he gradually added grey, green, black, and pink, as the sun came up. The last 16 prints are full of light and bold colors. And when all these prints went through numerous editions, different publishers and printers chose to accentuate the variety and contrasts between colors.

A purist, then, would prefer the earliest possible impression of each print, some of which seem almost silhouettes in blue, compared with later printings. Not me. I respect the blue, but I have chosen the most vividly colored prints from the public domain, and started with those. Why? I love color. But more, I find that the contrasts and highlights help clarify what we are looking at, and refresh the eye.

But to give a nod to the blue versions, I occasionally take a small detail, and invert the colors, which tends to bring out the black contour lines as white, and switches "realistic" colors for night-time glow.

Organizing

Whenever Hokusai came to a new location, he had to decide where to sit, how much of the scene to capture, what to ignore, what to emphasize. These compositional choices reflect a preference for scenes that offer many paths for attention to move through, different details that arouse our interest, opportunities to show numerous ordinary folks at work at their trades, oh, and natural beauty, too. A complex agenda, then, for an artist arranging the elements of the picture into a plausible representation of a real scene.

Consider the ways that Hokusai organizes those elements to intrigue our attention, to reward close examination, and to keep us exploring his picture, repeatedly. (There's real satisfaction to be had when our attention keeps being drawn through the picture along the same or similar paths, over and over.)

For example, he likes leading our eye on a zigzag trail back to Mount Fuji. We see samurai racing the horses along that kind of path through rice paddies, or winds blasting the peasants struggling along a similar levee. We follow along.

Often, he sets up a big event off center, whether it is a wave, a tree, or a boat. He likes strong diagonals, such as the gigantic beam that two men are sawing up into planks; it slashes across the page from the bottom right to the top left. He repeats some forms—the triangles of rooves of peasant huts, the rolling folds of grassy hills, the series of waves underneath a cargo boat, the thousand tiny marks that represent rice plants—without organizing them into neat rows. As the eye contemplates, picking up the similarity, the mind weaves all of them into a rough pattern—not symmetrical, but "natural," because the layout seems more like the way natural forms accrete.

In all these ways, Hokusai keeps our eyes a bit off balance, inquiring, seeking, discovering.

Contrast that with his patches of precision, which suggest that he is accurately reproducing the entire scene. He outlines the contours of forms with sharp, dark lines. His human figures, done with swift irregular lines, seem caught in the middle of an action, the caricatures given life by the dozens of lines showing knee, and hand, bend and back.

He sets the rolling curves of waves, hills, or clouds against the sharp straight lines and right angles of carefully detailed wooden structures—temples, shops, pleasure houses, viewing platforms, stacks of lumber. He clearly loves well-cut wood.

In one of his manuals for beginning painters, he recommends using a ruler—a straight edge—and in many pictures we see the perfectly parallel lines between every plank in the floor, the isometric view of a shop or tea warehouse, the slats of a window or a outside wall, the posts and walls of a country inn. He just loves architecture, as a subject—and a foil to play off against the deliberately irregular, apparently random, tree trunks, leaf clusters, forests, streams, rivers, and the open sea.

In these choices, Hokusai keeps us looking, as the mind seeks to resolve questions such as: where are we standing, as we look at this scene? How far is it to Mount Fuji, which we assume to be the farthest point we can see? How do human structures live within the natural world? And, in between, what are the humans doing down there, so tiny in this complex landscape?

My own preference is for a similar mix of the precise and the ambiguous. For example, I love pixels, zoomed way in, to show each colored square, but I take blocks of those to form a background, an interfering signal, an emotional mood. These patches have a double life—as computer-perfect squares but also, blurry smears of color.

But I am reacting to Hokusai's initial response. And because I am not primarily representing something in the real world, I drift toward symmetry as a way of organizing the dozen or so elements in my picture. I apologize if that makes it too easy to perceive.

Toward that end, I—and Hokusai—complexify the situation by adding text.

Texting

Hokusai inserts chunks of text throughout these prints, teasing us with the interplay of two forms of "reading."

The most obvious text elements appear within their own frame, appearing on top of the picture, separated from the image, but talking about it. For example, the signature gives a brief biography, pointing out that the creator has changed his artist name from the widely known "Hokusai" to "Iitsu," as in "Brush of Iitsu, the former Hokusai." The signature block, then, briefly breaks the illusion that we are just looking through a window at a real scene, reminding us that, yes, a bravura designer is at work here.

The second element within the signature block is the title. On the surface, this phrase tells us what location appears in the picture. But not so fast. Sometimes these titles are misleading; for example, when he announces that he is showing us the Seven Mile Beach in Sagami Province, he does not show us the beach.

Sometimes the title asserts a claim, but the scene is so unspecific that even his contemporaries could not point to a particular spot where he sketched. At other times he is drawing a popular tourist spot, but doing so from an unfamiliar vantage point, among the rooftops, say, so he needs to use the title to explain where we are. And many location names retain original meanings, giving a little touch of poetry to the scene; for example, Umezawa means, literally, a marsh full of plum trees. These are not simple labels.

Appearing within the picture (as contrasted with the way Western artists exclude their titles, relegating them to labels in the gallery) Hokusai's titles set off a subtle interplay between what we see and what it "means," between our first impression and multiple ways of interpreting the print.

Within the scene, Hokusai includes street names, teahouse signs, advertisements for products being sold, such as a special tea, official government notices on their own kiosk, even a description of a guardian deity on the back of a shrine. These texts give the scenes the air of real life, and veracity.

But he breaks the illusion by including the name or trademark of his publisher on a kite, on clothing, a hat, boxes being carried across a river. He even includes a full advertisement for the extended version, "New Edition of Thirty-Six Fuji in Stock." These marks and characters, easy to accept as just part of the scene, are, to the knowing customer, lowkey reminders of the commercial process that brings us these prints.

These prints, then, are very talkative. Hokusai once argued, in a manual called Quick Lessons in Simplified Drawing (1814) that because the brushstrokes that you learn to make in calligraphy are the same that you use in drawing, anyone who can write can draw. An exaggeration, no doubt, but an idea that he pursued in more than a thousand surimono, that is, works that combine a picture and a poem. Some of these were created collaboratively with contemporary poets to share in poetry clubs, and Hokusai's images take off from flowers, animals, seasons mentioned in the text, often obliquely illustrating or commenting on the text. Hokusai also created sets of prints about famous poets, showing what they looked like, and inserting part or all of one of their poems.

But in the 36 Views, he leaves out poetry. His tone is direct, empirical, practical; he is not reaching for overtones, spiritual suggestions, moral advice, or reminders of poems that formed part of the curriculum of a well-educated samurai or aristocrat. The texts that make it into these pictures are, or appear to be, "just the facts," about the scene, about himself, about the publication process, about commerce.

I have taken a more poetic approach, adding my own chunks of text to tell you what I think about the fragments of imagery that I have torn apart and reassembled. I interrupt your vision of the whole. I label, expand on what I see, cry out. My verbal elements obscure some of the underlying image, and in turn, some of the shadows below make the letters difficult to make out. Just as Hokusai is reflecting on what it means to view the mountain in the middle of the nation of Japan, I am pondering the experience of viewing him.

I offer multiple chunks of text and they can be read in any order, as the eye jumps around the image. In fact, I hope that different overtones and possible meanings arise as you tour the texts from one direction, then another. I first started doing this kind of "scattered" writing when I was in graduate school, perhaps under the influence of psychedelics. Several of these spatially laid-out and non-sequential poems ended up being published as "concrete poetry." In fact, a six-panel poem about Charles Ives became album notes for a record set. As with my hypertext experiments, I aim to offer multiple paths through the material, each path suggesting, hopefully, a slightly different perspective on the subject.

Circling Mount Fuji

Hokusai made landscape a valid subject for art in Japan. No more kabuki actors, mythical warriors, Zen monks. He'd done all those, before. Now he turned to the sights that were becoming popular with middle class tourists, landmarks that, when assembled in a series, showed the beauty and vitality of the nation, as defined in a new way—not as a feudal society, but a land full of workers, not a Kyoto of temples and palaces, but a natural land full of waterfalls, bridges, rivers, and, yes, that one big mountain, Mount Fuji.

A new attitude toward the notion of Japan, then…and a way to celebrate the visible, the tangible, the accessible. Not hidden palaces, or ancient texts, not even the warriors that Hokusai had so often portrayed when illustrating popular novels. A volcano, dormant under snow for three quarters of the year, available to pilgrims and tourists every summer—that was the symbol, the mark that Hokusai chose.

In his day, you could see Mount Fuji from Tokyo. Travelers bought guidebooks to the sights along the major highways that had been set up, long before, for the daimyos and their retainers to come serve the shogun. Hokusai saw the commercial possibilities of illustrating those scenic outlooks, those must-see views, and his competitors soon followed his path, doing their own series of prints on the natural wonders of the country. But Hokusai made Mount Fuji his trademark.

The advertisement for the **36 Views** boasted that "These pictures show the form of Fuji as it differs depending on the place, such as the shape seen from Shichirigahama, or the view observed from Tsukudajima: he has drawn them all so that none are the same." (Translation by Christine M. E. Guth, in "Hokusai's Great Waves in Nineteenth-Century Japanese Visual Culture," *The Art Bulletin*, Vol. 93, No. 4.)

The idea of circling around the mountain, too, is his. Like a string of prayer beads, his prints repeat that one mountain, the one constant in the middle of all the different vistas, and, at the same time, a shape shifter, growing taller then smaller, brighter or darker, white, red, bland or bright.

Mount Fuji had erupted in 1707, and might do so again; but for all its volatility, it was considered immortal. One popular etymology of its name traced "fuji" back to "fu-shi" meaning "no death." Pilgrims came every summer, making the climb, with the hope that they might attain immortality, or at least long life.

Did Hokusai subscribe to these beliefs, or did he just figure it was good luck to celebrate an emblem of the long life he hoped for, when he publicly planned his artistic progress up to the age 110?

Hokusai had long identified with the North Star, as the embodiment of the Boddhi-sattva Myōken. One night, after spending three weeks in a retreat at her temple, he emerged during a storm, and was struck by lightning. He recovered, and believed his survival was due to her intervention. He is said to have recited her mantra continuously as he walked around the city. All his artist names refer, in one way or another, to her.

To have a miraculous redeemer, whose emblem was an immovable presence in the constantly changing night sky, what did this mean for Hokusai? It seems, at least as a form of spiritual practice, that he was concentrating on a single point, as he moved around.

Perhaps Mount Fuji served as a similar symbol to concentrate on, to bring good luck, blessing, and immortality.

To perform some spiritual practices such as reciting a mantra, focusing on a single point, or sharpening the attention, one must stay in the "now." And Hokusai's pictures give that impression. We get the feeling that we are witnessing a living moment. Not a religious mood, not a worship of a far-off being, but a real, tangible, visible fact, around which a whole moment can turn.

Making an impression

Hokusai borrowed techniques from Western prints and Chinese art, but he does not seem to have intended his work for export. Yet his prints quickly became shorthand for Japan around the world, more popular than the more subtle screens and scrolls made by the literati, the Zen monks, and the artists trained in traditional schools.

Twenty years after his death, Hokusai's prints were at the center of a craze for all things Japanese, *Japonisme*, which seems to have started in France after the United States opened Japan up for trade. Paris then saw a flood of imports and exhibitions bringing ukiyo-e prints, kimonos, Buddhas, scrolls, fans, and other exotic goods that appealed to critics like the Goncourt brothers, novelists such as Zola, and artists such as Manet.

And, led by Claude Monet, the Impressionists seized on Hokusai and Hiroshige for alternatives to the slick, dead conventions of the French Academy.

Just as Hokusai grabbed some techniques from the Dutch prints that were being brought into Japan in the 18th century, Monet and his group felt encouraged in their own experiments by what they discovered in Hokusai and the other ukiyo-e artists.

What practices did Hokusai encourage among the Impressionists?

- Taking contemporary life as a subject: crowds in the city, real people out in the countryside (as opposed to shepherds and nymphs in pastoral never-never lands)

• Working out doors in the open air, so that images contained more natural light than the dim shadows of a studio, so weather became part of the scene. Hokusai sketched on the spot, but built his pictures in the studio using those sketches to create a scene that looked as if it had been created on location. Monet went much farther in working right in the motif, though he retouched afterward, and later in his life, created some canvases purely in the studio. For both artists, though, the goal was to give us the illusion of seeing a real scene, out in the open, not a fantasy worked up indoors.

• Making each brushstroke visible: Hokusai's innumerable marks, dabs, dashes—indicating, variously, rice plants, trees, hills, or waves—encouraged these impressionists to leave their own brushwork visible, rather than smoothing it over as the Academy recommended.

• Using bright colors to catch the attention of viewers, tired of the dark browns and varnished shadows that the Academy equated with beauty.

• Scaling down: unlike the gigantic canvases that won imperial or ecclesiastical awards, the smaller, more portable canvases used by the Impressionists found an odd justification in the small ukiyo-e prints, both aiming at a middle class audience of artisans, merchants, professionals, in their apartments and homes, rather than the wealthy with their palaces, and the state, with its grand buildings.

• Touring: the idea that an image could help city dwellers envision a scene that they might like to visit on a weekend, and the sense that a series of prints could give you a tour around a major landmark, may have helped Monet justify his own travels around France, and his multiple views of its cathedrals, valleys, cliffs, haystacks, and rivers.

Of course, influence can be exaggerated. Some problems that the Impressionists were trying to solve would have seemed alien to Hokusai—how to capture the multiple colors that show up in shadows, for example, or how to represent the irregular shapes and changing colors of ripples and waves. These challenges could only be addressed in oil paint, something that Hokusai never touched. A print, even one with several layers of overprinting, cannot show such subtleties.

Hokusai, then, was not an Impressionist, but many avant-garde French critics and artists mis-appropriated his work as an exotic but understandable justification for a constellation of practices and ideas that were grouped loosely under that rubric. And that raises the question: In what ways did Hokusai make his work amenable to this interpretation?

Yes, each print seems like it captures a moment—a fleeting impression of a particular place at a specific time of day, in a particular season, with its own wind, rain, or mist. We see people tilting forward, taking a step, holding a bucking horse, carrying buckets of tea leaves—almost no one is at rest in a Hokusai. The wind lifts a kite and twists its tail. The porters splash across a river, bearing the daimyo and his luggage. Nothing is at rest. Hence, the impression that we are seeing an instant. If cameras had been invented, we might call these scenes photographic.

But each picture is a personal reinvention of the scene. Hokusai violates the laws of perspective at times by making a distant person larger than a nearby one. He assembles half a dozen people as if they all just happened to be walking by at the same time—though I suspect each individual figure, sketched on the spot, gets dropped into the picture to give us his own personal impression of busy human activity.

So an impression can also be artificial, as when we say someone is trying to make an impression on us. Hokusai relies on the conventions of both Chinese and Japanese art to represent objects that are impossible to represent in the tools he had available—lines and marks like those in calligraphy, and solid blocks of color, caught in a motionless print.

Real waves, for instance, swell with a gradient of colors, changing as they move, folding as they trip over the rising beach, receding—all that activity gets frozen into claw-like fractals in Hokusai's wave off Kanagawa.

Similarly, evanescent, amorphous, moving clouds get turned into white blocks that just sit still in the print, blocking our view of whatever lies below.

Real rice plants are green, but get represented by innumerable little black slash marks. We "read" these conventional representations well enough; we accept the translation from the real to the metaphorical, while recognizing that, well, this is a summary, not a full representation. In that sense, we accept these aspects of the picture as "just" an impression.

In all these ways, then, Hokusai's art makes an impression on us; the images capture our attention, exercise it by drawing us through the landscape over and over, discovering new information as we go, leaving the overall "impression" in our brain.

And the art is literally made on a press, because professional wood carvers laid Hokusai's sketches on blocks of cherry, and cut his lines in the wood, making an impression on that block, which then served as the bed on which the printer laid mulberry paper, and pressed down, to make the final impression.

In my work, I create on the computer, and print on aluminum. Today's printing processes allow me to capture the full range of colors, and the 300 pixels per inch resolution, so that the image that emerges has more than 64,000 hues available, and lines as thin as one pixel width. For me, then, printing is not nearly as limiting as it was for Hokusai. But I cannot pretend to be sketching a scene in 19th century Japan. My pieces are aggressively artificial: disassembling the original Hokusai print, rebuilding it, inserting my commentary, arguing with the dead, interacting with images, not real people or mountains. I am giving you my "impression" of Hokusai, asserting that my pictures are conversations, not final statements.

Because this is a conversation, I look forward to hearing what you think.
—Jonathan Reeve Price

FAQ

Where are you coming from?

At 79 I am an emerging artist for the second time. Once again, I have limited resources, few contracts, big ideas.

Back in the 1970's, I did public art and concrete poetry. I painted the 64 hexagrams of the I Ching on a quarter mile of the elevated Westside Highway, along the Hudson River in New York. This roadway had been closed to traffic after a repair truck, full of hot tar, broke through and fell onto cars below. Sneaking up there in the early mornings, I used the cobblestone grid to lay out the straight and broken lines, color-coding them for the trigrams—Earth, Sky, Lake, Mountain, Water, Thunder, Fire, and the Valley. In the gallery, you got photos of the finished work, and a map, so you could go out, ride your bike along King Wen's images, and, when you felt the moment, stop to find your fortune.

My texts appeared in posters all around Soho, where I was living in a loft, back when artists were transforming the warehouses and sweatshops into livable spaces, and artists' coops. My ice cream cone poem, a tribute to Claes Oldenburg's canvas sculptures, appeared first in a poster designed by Joel Katz, then got reproduced in a bunch of anthologies. Other texts appeared on inflatable weather balloons, video art pieces, and in the gallery, as panels with words that evoke colors, in An Alphabet in the Spectrum of the Rainbow.

Now I am not so public. I make limited editions of aluminum prints exploring USGS maps of our rivers and borders, photos of the bosque and acequia of the Southwest, and digital remakes of famous pictures, such as those of Hokusai.

I love data. In my many years creating content for high tech companies in Silicon Valley, Tokyo, Los Alamos, and Albuquerque, I've learned to cherish entity relationship diagrams, taxonomies, thesauri, relational and object-oriented databases, and code. Pixels are my pals. So I delve into the image, uncovering the "real" behind the illusion—I surface pixels, code, and false color, to get some distance from the "veracity" claimed by engineers, and the "truth" suggested by Hokusai.

To get free of mere data, then, I turn to imagination—the holy. In this crucible we heat up images that drive us forward—extending or denying empathy, conceiving of what others may be feeling, or shutting them out, as subhuman, alien.

So what is new in my attitude, compared to what I thought back in the 70's? Spirit, love, and extension. I have a broader reach now. I see more than formal perspectives in art, and my approach is, ironically, more emotional, intuitive, and soft than my hard-edged, rather intellectual approach, when I was making conceptual posters through-out Soho, or publishing concrete poems, where the text mirrored the shape of the subject, like an ice cream cone. Perhaps it helps that I haven't taken acid for more than 40 years. Those revelations opened me up. But time and spiritual work have let me consolidate and unfold. I hope you enjoy the results. If you feel the impulse, let me know what you think, at JonathanReevePrice@gmail.com. No guarantees, but I might reply.

What are some of your solo shows?

- *Acequia*, Los Ranchos Town Hall, Los Ranchos, NM.
- *Alphabet in the Spectrum of the Rainbow*, West Broadway Gallery, NY.
- *Balloon Poems*, Cooper Union, New York, NY.
- *Canvas Photos*, Verle II Gallery, Hartford, CT.
- *Edible I Ching*, Soho Gallery, New York, NY.
- *Flophouse Follies*, with Joel Katz. Hopkins Center, Dartmouth College, Hanover, NH.
- *I Ching on the West Side Highway, 18th to 23rd Streets*, New York, NY, West Broadway Gallery, New York, NY.
- *Liquid Border,* Gallery with a Cause, Albuquerque, NM.
- *Paste Ups*, West Broadway Gallery, New York, NY.
- *Rio Grande: Wetlands/Borderlands*, Open Space Center, Albuquerque, NM.

Where have you been in group shows?

- 311 Gallery, Raleigh, NC.
- Art League Rhode Island, Providence, RI.
- Avant-Garde Festival, New York, NY.
- Boston Visual Artists' Union, Boston, Massachusetts.
- Brooklyn Museum, Brooklyn, NY.
- Cade Art Gallery, Anne Arundel Community College, Arnold, MD
- Center of the Arts, Tubac, AZ.

- Farmington Museum, Farmington, NM.
- Fort Works Art, Fort Worth, TX.
- Grey Art Gallery, New York University, NY.
- Henry Hicks Gallery, Brooklyn, New York.
- Kensington Arts Association, Toronto, Ontario, Canada
- Librije Beeldende Kunst, Utrecht, Holland.
- Loeb Student Center, New York University, New York, NY.
- Mississippi State University Art Gallery, MS.
- Museum of Parc Mont Royal, Montreal, Quebec, Canada.
- New Mexico Art League, Albuquerque, NM.
- Pleiades Gallery, New York, NY.
- Richmond Museum, Norfolk, VA.
- Sangre de Cristo Arts Center, Pueblo, CO.
- Site: Brooklyn, Brooklyn, NY.
- West Broadway Gallery, New York, NY.
- Whitney Counterweight,. Soho, NY.
- Women's Caucus of Colorado, Lakewood, CO.

Any museums?

Seventeen pieces from this set have been taken for the permanent collections of the Albuquerque Museum, and the Rumsey Map Collection of Stanford University.

Other works have appeared in group shows at the Jewish Museum, and the Brooklyn Museum, in New York.

Who's reviewed your art?

- *American Artist*
- *Art News*
- *Artists Review Art*
- *Arts Magazine*
- *Christian Science Monitor*
- *Kirkus Reviews*
- *New York Magazine*
- *New York Times*
- *Soho Weekly News*
- *The Nation*

- *Village Voice*
- *Women Artists' Newsletter*

Where can we find some of your poems?

Here are some anthologies with my (mostly) concrete poetry.
- *Sounds and Silences, Poetry for Now*, edited by Richard Peck, Delacorte, and Dell Books, New York, 1970
- *Imaged Words and Worded Images*, edited by Richard Kostelanetz, Outerbridge and Dienstfrey, New York, NY, 1970.
- *Future Fictions*, Panache, Princeton, NJ, 1971.
- *In Youth*, edited by Richard Kostelanetz, Ballantine Books, New York, 1972.
- *Concrete is Not Always Hard*, edited by A. Barbara Pilon, Xerox Educational Publications, Middletown, Connecticut, 1972.
- *Contemporary Poetry in America*, edited by Miller Williams, Random House, NY, 1973.
- *Media Mix*, edited by Alec Allinson, Beverley Allinson, and John McInnes, Thomas Nelson and Sons, Don Mills, Ontario, 1973.
- *Visual Literature Criticism: A New Collection*, edited by Richard Kostelanetz, Southern Illinois University Press, Carbondale, IL, 1979.
- *Literature of Work*, Edited by Sheila E, Murphy, John G. Sperling, and John D. Murphy, University of Phoenix Press, Phoenix, Az, 1991.
- *The Poetry of Business Life: An Anthology*, edited by Ralph Windle, Berrett-Koehler Publishers, San Francisco, CA 1994.
- *Essaying Essays: Alternative Forms of Exposition*, edited by Richard Kostelanetz, Out of London Press, New York, NY, 2012.

What are some books you've written?

- *The Liquid Border: The Rio Grande from El Paso to the Gulf of Mexico*, Communication Circle, 2020.
- *Write a Use Case: Gathering Requirements that Users can Understand*, Communication Circle, 2020.
- *American Scenery: Thomas Cole vs NASA*, Communication Circle, 2019.
- *Remapping Paris, A MuseumZero Exhibition*, Communication Circle, 2018.

- *Get Past the Tags: How to Write (and Read) XML*, Communication Circle, 2018.
- *Hot Text—Web Writing that Works!* With Lisa Price, Peachpit Pearson, 2002.
- *Digital Imaging: The Official HP Guide,* with Lisa Price, IDG Books, 1999.
- *Outlining Goes Electronic: A Study of the Impact of Media on our Understanding of the Role of Outlining in Virtual and Collaborative Conversations.* ATTW Series, Ablex, 1999.
- *The Virtual Playhouse for the Macintosh,* Hayden Books, 1994.
- *How to Communicate Technical Information*, with Henry Korman, Adam Rochmes, Linda Urban, and Mick Renner. Benjamin/Cummings. 1993.
- *Classic Scenes.* New American Library, 1979.
- *The Best Thing on TV: Commercials.* Viking Press, Penguin Books, 1978.
- *Video Visions: A Medium Discovers Itself.* New American Library, 1977.
- *Life Show: How to See Theater in Life and Life in Theater,* with John Lahr. Viking Press and Penguin Books. 1973. Reissued by Limelight Editions, 1990.
- *On Finnegans Wake* (pamphlet). Grove Press. 1972.
- *Critics on Robert Lowell* (editor). University of Miami Press, U.K. edition: Allen and Unwin. 1972.

Where can we go to learn more about you?

Blog: http://museumzero.blogspot.com/
Linked In: http://www.linkedin.com/in/JonathanReevePrice
Amazon Author Page: https://www.amazon.com/author/jonathanprice
Web site: MuseumZero.Art

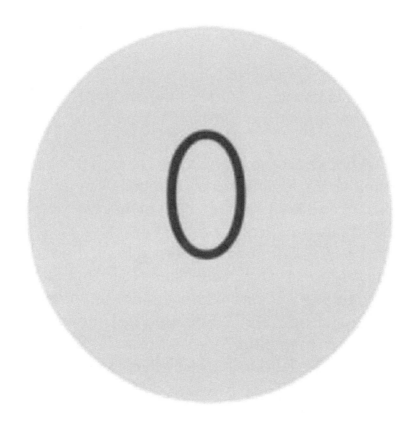

The Communication Circle, LLC
Publishers of Fine Art Books
4704 Mi Cordelia Drive, NW
Albuquerque, NM 87120
(505) 259-7937
MuseumZero.art

Made in the USA
Las Vegas, NV
16 February 2023

67647037R00045